love
AFTER
Cancer

A JOURNEY THROUGH

Hope

Empowerment

Affirmation

Transformation

AN INTERACTIVE JOURNAL TO HELP TELL YOUR STORY

Table of Contents

PART III: YOUR JOURNEY RECORDED

Acknowledgements

I first want to thank God for speaking in me and through me to write this book. It is through God's grace that I have the words to bless others. I am so grateful for the assignment to be a vessel, servant and a steward, imparting empowerment into the lives of countless women and men.

I want to thank my parents, Lenard George Washington Carter and LaTanya Rose Denard-Johnson. It is because of them that I have life and it is because of them that I live. My purpose is driven by their prayers for me. The initial release date of this project was the weekend my dad passed on up to the heavens, 4/15/2018. Now, he will not get to physically read my book, but I believe his spirit has carried me through to the end and I know he's seeing it now from above. His strength and love are felt through the thread of my words, every breath I take and every move I make. My mom, my first Rose, has supported me and has kept my creative drive going strong. Both of my parents have numerous talents that have been engraved in my DNA and I am so grateful that I am able to carry it out and be a part of their lineage.

God blessed me with another dad, Verma Johnson, who has been instrumental in showing me how to use life lessons to be a stronger and well-rounded woman. It's in our long and sometimes debate-driven, conversations that I have grown and changed my perspective on life and myself.

My understanding and compassionate daughter has been patient with me throughout the course of me putting this project together, among other things. My gift from God, Kristyna Rose, is simply amazing. She has inspired me to continue even when I didn't feel like it. It's because of her that I force myself past any storm in my life, in hopes that she will know that she can do exceedingly and abundantly above all she could ever ask, think, or imagine according to the strong power of God operating in and through her (Ephesians 3:20).

To my siblings, Derrick Carter, Dwayne Carter, Dr. Erika Rolle, Akeem Carter, Keenan Denard, Trina Baker, and Vermetra Jackson, you all mean the world to me. I thank God for your support, encouragement, prayers, and for keeping me in check. We shall rise up and take over the world.

I am grateful for my survivor sister, Teal Diva—Shannon Routh—for always giving me a chance and an opportunity to share my gifts with the world. It is because of her, the Teal Diva Survivor Retreats, and her belief in me when I didn't believe in myself that this book has been produced. It has been from every retreat, trip, and event that the words from God were placed in my heart, placed on paper, now to be revealed to the world.

I am forever thankful for my doctors, nurses, technicians and secretaries who have been with me along this journey before, during, and in my life after cancer. Your caring hearts, prayers, love and support have not gone unnoticed. *Thank you.*

I am appreciative to God for Pastors, John and Elaine Lofton for assisting my spiritual growth and support when I was in a vulnerable place in my life. I appreciate your feedback on this project. I am grateful that my Rose and I get the full C-3—Covenant Community Church—experience. We have witnessed the display of true kingdom family, true teaching of the Word, authentic love and compassion.

I am humbled by God for my accountability partner and A.B., Ericka Rhodes, who understands me, walks me through countless days and nights through my mess and challenges me to go bigger and be better, and to boldly and confidently share my message.

I praise God for Eric Coffie who kept me from a poverty mindset, challenging me to be greater.

I have sincere gratitude for the myriad of other mothers who have imparted their wisdom into my life and displayed for me what boldness and true womanhood looks like. Also, to my teal sisters, who have gifted me with their strength, courage, advice and love, which has anchored me to persist on my course in life.

Last, but certainly not least, I want to recognize my TEAM. Sponsors Ericka Rhodes and Shirley Johnson; Serenity, Courage & Wisdom, Inc. board members and volunteers; my assistants, Wala'a and Karin; graphics and photography designers, Hibiscus Brand Management and Metrolina Media; my super awesome editor, Elaine Garcia from Before You Publish; Melissa Brown-Jenkins; my Profit Lady, Shontaye Hawkins; and The Real Profit Club.

Anyone else I may have missed that has contributed to me being who I am today and have had a hand in me giving birth to this book, *thank you.*

Dedication

It is as Lilly Singh once said in an interview, "I am appreciative to the woman that I have yet to meet. The one who I am working hard to eventually see. The one who scares me, but I know I must strive for because I have a mini me who I am a model for."

So, this is for her. To empower her to come forth. As she will eventually appear as I will not give up until she does.

To the person I am becoming.

Foreword

Being diagnosed with cancer changes a person. Sometimes, you are introduced to a person you never knew existed. This person lives deep inside of you; like an alter ego.

I met Keesha in 2010. We had both been diagnosed with a gynecologic cancer. Our paths crossed at several community events that honored cancer survivors. My first impression of Keesha was that she was a super sweet person who had a strong faith; she had a love of all things sparkly and she had some big ideas for life after cancer. All of this was a quick recipe for friendship for the two of us.

For the first few years of our friendship, we shared ideas and frustrations. We shared our most vulnerable moments and came to know each other's family. The Keesha I got to know had big ideas. This Keesha was going places. This Keesha was also scared. Shy. Vulnerable. And, at times, unsure of herself.

When Keesha steps on a stage, or anywhere she is sharing her creative journey, she immediately becomes La Luz, or The Light, and I saw this from the first time I heard Keesha share her story. This was a different Keesha. This Keesha was bold. Passionate. Stimulating. Ambitious. Creative. This Keesha was a stunner. A showstopper.

This is the Keesha you are going to meet in the following pages. She will take you on a journey from when she was diagnosed, to her loss of creativity and love for writing, to the woman she is today and strives to become.

On numerous occasions, I have had the privilege of watching her transform lives. Through my non-profit, Teal Diva, she has conducted journaling workshops at our survivor retreats and performed on stage for one of our events, *Cooking for a Cause,* where she moved and inspired everyone, ending in a standing ovation.

Keesha recognizes that there is power in the words we use and in sharing our personal stories. She is gifted in, not only sharing her story, but also teaching other cancer survivors how to share their stories through various workshops she conducts.

Keesha is more than a friend to me. She is my mentor. My advisor. My peer. My partner. My soul sister. I have had the unique pleasure of watching Keesha through the years shed her pre-cancerous skin and become a bold woman, sure of her direction: standing up to cancer and purposefully pursuing her new life.

Ladies and gentleman, it is my pleasure to introduce you to Keesha "La Luz" Carter in "Love After Cancer: A Journey Through Hope, Empowerment, Affirmation, & Transformation."

Shannon Routh

Founder & CEO, Teal Diva

TealDiva.org

Introduction

I would have never imagined a life that included the word—Cancer. You would not have told me that I would be an author sharing my cancer survivor story. In my mind, my book was supposed to be a totally different memoir with a drastically different outcome. Not as a single mother who had been promised that she would never be able to birth a child again. Being robbed of a simple event such as childbirth is one of the many events during my life after cancer that has changed me. It is my story, not a pity party.

I dream of having a life I would never want to escape from. I still have some ways to go and pray that time remains on my side. In years to come, my expectation is that my life will continue to fill me with joy and smiles.

Throughout my life after cancer, overthrowing the enemy in me—my mindset—seems so much harder to conquer, than overcoming cancer. However, I know that just as I trained my brain in ways that blew people's mind while going through treatment, I know I can condition my mind to do the same with the trials of life. Using my thoughts and imagination to bring peace and joy during tumultuous seasons in life empowers me. I now know, when life throws a curve ball that may knock me off kilter, I can maintain dynamite mindset power that will position me to stand firm and be fierce and unstoppable.

This collection of writings, done over the past six years, reveals a glimpse into my reality. My mindset.

My heart. The thoughts that I kept deep down inside my soul. Thoughts that only God and I knew about.

As you read this book, escape with me to a world of a cancer diagnosis that many know all too well. It's a place I would never want you to live, and a place hard to understand, unless you have lived it yourself. Sometimes it's a lonely place, because the responses from the world show the lack of knowledge of what it is really like. It's not until you connect with someone who has worn your shoes—the same size shoe—someone who knows exactly what it feels like, how it moves, how it glides. Then, and only then, do you feel a relief and a piece of freedom to be *YOU*. Free to be your authentic self in all of your strengths and insecurities. Free to be bolder and walk into the person you were created to become. Free to be the soldier that is equipped with everything that is needed to *WIN*. Take a chance today and *walk in your divine destiny*.

Someone once said, *"She was unstoppable, not because she did not have failures or doubts, but because she continued on despite them."* Let this story be about *YOU*.

Excelsior. Excelsior. Continue onward and upward. Share your story and live your authentic life. No matter what.

~Keesha "La Luz" Carter

PART I:

LOVE AFTER CANCER

Chapter 1

"You don't always need a plan. Sometimes you just need to breathe, trust, let go and see what happens." – Mandy Hale

June 2008, I headed to Wingate, North Carolina with change on my mind. I left Miami, Florida looking for a new life with my daughter, Kristyna Rose. Everything started off shaky. After having an unexpected interview that I entered feeling quite intimidated, the job promised to me was given to someone else.

I had never interviewed in a room with more than three people. Here, it was at least four or five. I had to perform and I did not feel comfortable. It felt as though they knew whom they wanted before I arrived and that played over and over again in my head. I didn't show up with confidence as I should have. What I learned then, and a few times over since, is that you will have moments of opportunity in life that will just happen, and you'd better be ready. *Just breathe.*

The other thing I learned, which I was unaware of at the time, is that not getting that job was a blessing in disguise. Five months later, I was taking a series of antibiotics that led me to question my doctor about my health.

Prior to moving to North Carolina, I was diagnosed with the Human Papillomavirus, also known as HPV. My previous doctors (in Miami) said, although I had been diagnosed with the virus, I was fine. My last appointment was the week I moved to North Carolina and I asked them if I was okay. Again, I was reassured. No problems. So, of course, I thought I had no worries. Here again, another lesson learned. I did not do a lot of research at the time on what HPV was. It was a fairly new discovery and studies were just being released about it and its vaccines.

At the end of 2008, I had back-to-back sinus infections. I was on antibiotics over and over, which was abnormal for me. It stood out to me as something odd. So, when a bacterial infection rose up, I knew I needed to get checked on a much deeper level. When I told my new doctor to check me from the roota to the toota, it was to both of our surprise what happened next.

I was hopeful, unaware, completely blindsided, and thrown a curve ball by what I thought would be an ordinary physical examination. One that would literally change my life forever. As my primary care physician, Dr. Laguerre, conducted my Pap test, he repeatedly asked in a voice of major concern, when I'd had my last pap exam.

I looked at him in confusion as my interest in this repeated question became alarming because I kept giving the same answer, "The first week in June 2008."

He'd reply, "Are you sure?"

"Yes, I'm sure."

He would look down between my legs, and then I could see his head pop back up with a puzzled look and he would ask me again. What kept going through my mind was, *What's happening? What's going on? Why does he keep looking down there, then popping back up to ask me the same questions again and again? Why is he leaving the room with a puzzled look on his face?*

Dr. Laguerre's facial expressions were that of shock, concern, and appall as he left the room. He eventually asked for his female colleague to come and examine me. She must have confirmed his suspicions. He had found a mass.

Doctors are pretty good at not showing when they have found something traumatic. He took tests. Asked me questions and mentioned that he was concerned. He didn't want to make any claims on what it was; but said it could be just a fibroid tumor that could be removed with surgery. It looked to be the size of a quarter, however, he did not know for sure. He agreed with me when I said I hoped that was all it was. He then asked me to immediately go to a hospital nearby to get a vaginal ultrasound and that he was scheduling me for an appointment to see a gynecologist.

This would be the beginning of a series of doctors, nurses and technicians looking at, probing and examining my vagina.

I'm not going to lie, I was concerned and bewildered. It was the first time anything major happened to my body outside of having my daughter in a natural childbirth; and that was with no epidural. I went to the hospital and they put the Transvaginal Transducer, that would view my pelvic area, inside of my vagina. I wished at that moment I could see something on the technician's face. Nothing.

I went home puzzled and confused. I prayed, "Lord, I hope it's nothing major." Here I am, 27 years old, about to turn 28, a single mother with visions of a promising future for my daughter and I. Everything had abruptly stopped with millions of questions running through my mind.

Since I didn't get the job I came to North Carolina for, I constantly searched and searched for work with nothing coming about. Anyone in this position can relate to the frustration and anxiety of wondering how you will provide for you and your family. What I knew I needed to do was believe and know that everything was going to work out for our good. *Just trust.*

I eventually took a seasonal job at Pier 1 Imports in the fall of 2008 to help carry me over. Bills were coming in and I needed for my daughter and me to survive. After the season was over, early 2009, I secured employment at a child daycare center where I worked with 3-year-olds.

I would get so caught up in my lessons, and working with the children, and get totally lost in what I was doing. Any and everything outside of that building was a blur until it was time for me to leave.

During this time, Dr. Laguerre had scheduled a major appointment for me with a gynecologist several times. However, I kept missing the appointments so, when Dr. Laguerre called me while I was at work and told me that this was serious, and I needed not miss the next appointment, my heart dropped. At this point, I had not been told about the c word. I knew then, this was not to be taken lightly for my doctor to call me at work and express his concern. He also mentioned that I would be dropped as a patient if I did not make the next appointment.

When I arrived, the doctor checked me, and then he looked me in my face with concern, saying that it looked like I had cancer on my cervix.

Huh? What do you mean? Are you sure this is not a fibroid? Come on now, I can handle that, but cancer? No, I don't know that I can handle that. I can't believe the words that are coming out of your mouth right now. These thoughts ran through my mind. *Just see what happens.*

Chapter 2

"Cancer does not have a face until it's yours or someone you know." – Anthony Del Monte

I was determined to arrive on time, as I had to travel an hour to Presbyterian Hospital where I was to meet my obstetrics and gynecologic (OBGYN) oncologist. I came to get a second opinion and to find out if, indeed, I had cancer. It was cold. Not only was it cold inside the hospital, but also within me. As I found my way through the unfamiliar halls, while people scurrying around me heading to their appointed destinations, I thought to myself, *What a way to start the day.* My heart was cold as I held my breath waiting to be seen, curious of his findings, praying and asking God for this suspense to end with a positive outcome.

I had traveled there alone. It was one of those appointments where I had to make sure to leave work on time to drive an hour away. I sure did not want to miss another appointment, nor did I want to live another day in suspense. I wanted to know if this thing in me was a fibroid or the c word.

Everyone was so nice—my nurse—my doctor. They took me through the normal routine like any other doctor appointment. Again, I undressed from the waist down. I felt so cheap, like I had been standing on 79th Street in Miami, giving private, intimate parts of me away. The difference here was that I was paying for it and there was no pleasure in it for those on the other side or for me.

So, as done several times before, my oncologist, Dr. McDonald, examined my vagina, and then left the room. But, this time he returned and confirmed it to be true—I had what is called Squamous Cell Carcinoma, a type of cervical cancer. Stage II B, to be exact.

My God. Was he sure? I'd just met him, and now he was telling me that cancer was in my body. Geesh. What happened next was just as shocking.

Dr. McDonald informed me that he would be the one to conduct all future pap examinations. He cleared his schedule to sit and talk with me in detail. He said I could contact my mom (who was an hour away) to come join in the consultation. I found this odd, as my previous doctors in Miami were always overbooked and never cleared their calendars to sit and have a consultation at the spur of a moment. When my mother arrived, Dr. McDonald answered our questions and explained in detail what was going on inside my new changed body with this invader—cancer. He went over our options and suggested I get a second opinion if I desired.

Of course, I wanted to; after all, he was recommending that I needed a hysterectomy. I never had surgery before and didn't want to have it then. The size of the cancer was too large for me to just have a cone procedure, which is where they cut off part of the cervix—that's what I wanted. I prayed for the cone. I prayed for this to be done and over with.

So, this led my mom and me north to Chapel Hill, North Carolina. I felt good about this medical research facility. I was confident that they would give me either news of me being able to get the cone procedure or confirm what Dr. McDonald had said: a complete hysterectomy.

Hey, after all, I wanted to one day get married and have at least one more child.

At this appointment, I saw two doctors. One was a student resident, and the other, a senior OBGYN oncologist. They both confirmed what Dr. McDonald had previously shared. The cancerous area was too large for me to be a candidate for the cone procedure. In fact, with my legs up, with a shining light, my mother was able to see the cancer as she peered down into my vagina, into the tunnel that lead to the home of the serial killer, known as cervical cancer. With her naked eye, she could see that it had invaded my body.

This was the onset of war in my mind—*The Enemy in Me*—as thoughts raced through my mind.

The thoughts would not stop. I searched and searched online for any information, so much that my mother told me, "Stop looking at that stuff online. You are going to make yourself crazy."

I looked up the type of cancer I had. I looked up ways to beat it. Natural ways. Natural foods. I wanted to win. I didn't want to be defeated because I had a future and a plan for my daughter and me. I knew there was more. There had to be more. I was scared. I was strong. Then, I was mad. I was confused. I felt raped. I felt betrayed. One thing was for certain, I didn't want to go forward not knowing and understanding this time, as to what was growing and going on in my body. *No, not this time.*

As I searched the World Wide Web for answers, I also waited for my surgery to take place, which was exactly a month later. *Surgery?* This was nerve-wracking because I had never been put to sleep or had my body cut on. Nothing besides my daughter splitting my vagina during childbirth. Dr. McDonald informed my mother and I that surgery would be scheduled, and he would check my lymph nodes to see if the cancer had begun to spread. If so, he would recommend chemotherapy and radiation.

Oh, no. I did not want to go through that. I prayed to the Lord for this cancer not to be in my lymph nodes. I wasn't quite sure what to expect, but I eventually surrendered and gave my fears and concerns to God.

It helped when my sister, Erika, flew in from Miami for the surgery. She gave me a bracelet with a cross on it that someone had given to her that was prayed over. I held it in my hand and prayed all the way to the point when they had to take it away before I went into surgery.

I visualized God's presence as they prepped me for surgery. As the nurse searched for my veins to start my IV, I tried everything in my power not to be anxious. This was the beginning of me activating faith. Faith that

I didn't know I had. This was me learning to operate in the strength that was stored up deep down inside of my soul and me.

Chapter 3

"Sometimes you have to forget what's gone, appreciate what still remains, and look forward to what's coming next." – *Will Smith*

Once the surgery was over, I woke up to Erika and my mother sitting in the hospital room with me. They stared at me with dazed expressions that I could not interpret. I asked how the surgery had gone, but they didn't want to tell me. They said, "Let's wait for the doctor so he can explain it to you."

Questions began running through my head. *Was the cancer in my lymph nodes? Did I have a hysterectomy, or not?* I begged them to tell me. I wanted some peace of mind. Laying in the hospital bed, with the door on my left and the window on my right, was one of the stillest moments in time. My stomach was tight. The only thoughts in my head were that, *I want to live.*

Finally, they gave in and shared the news with me. The doctor found cancer in my lymph nodes. So, I heard his voice repeat in my head that if there was cancer in my lymph nodes, he would keep my organs in tack, which meant no hysterectomy. Then, he would recommend chemo and radiation because it worked better with my organs in place. Still a little out of it from the surgery, I lay there with a strength that came from a place that was unfamiliar to me.

I said, "Okay, what's next? Where do we go from here?" My mind tuned into healing. I didn't know how, I just knew that there was more life for me.

I prayed...

Dr. McDonald entered the room. He was tall, redhead, peaceful and with his calm spirit, he confirmed the words that my sister and mother had stated. He added that he moved my ovaries up to protect them, but he couldn't promise they would not be impacted by the radiation. He also said the unimaginable. I had graduated now to stage III cervical cancer due to it spreading beyond my cervix, into my lymph nodes.

What's next? were the words that filled my mind.

He explained that he would schedule me for chemo and radiation to begin in four weeks. I was hoping for more time, so I could heal more from the surgery, but he assured me everything was going to be fine.

Once I was home healing from surgery, it was tough trying to explain this process to my two-year-old. It broke my heart every time she looked at me. She would observe me in bewilderment when I would tell her I couldn't lift her. When I told her that she could not come near my belly, she just stared at me in confusion and it only got worse once treatment started. Talk about post-partum depression. I cried a lot of days. I felt helpless.

Now, two years later, I felt helpless again because I felt like I couldn't give her the affection she sought after. Then chemo and radiation came. With the side effects, I slept a lot and would feel so nauseous. When she wanted to bounce and roll around in the bed, I had to stop her joy and excitement to tell her to take it to the floor, so I could bare it. This hurt my heart. I had to look at a youthful and playful child in the face and try to smile when I was crying inside. Praying that I would live to enjoy her for many more years to come. I prayed...

Chapter 4

"The mystery of human existence lies not in just staying alive, but in finding something to live for." – Fyodor Dostoyevsky

My first day of chemo and radiation they explained how things would go. Mondays would be my longer days. Getting the *drip, drip, drip* of chemotherapy took hours. In the beginning, I had my mind made up that I was going to cut my hair off after my first appointment. I asked about my hair coming out, and I was reassured that it would not come out due to the type and levels of chemotherapy I would be taking. The *drip, drip, drip* I took was called Cisplatin. To my surprise, I didn't lose my hair. In fact, my hair on my head seemed to get stronger. I don't know why, but it remained. I can't say the same about below my waist.

Being a hairy woman before treatment, to now barely growing hair on my legs was such a shock. I didn't complain.

I was becoming familiar with my newfound routine. After my long eight hours, or so, of chemotherapy, I was then introduced to the radiation machine. There was a Sirius Radio-like system that played while I laid down to receive the radiation. The huge machine rotated around my body and I would lie there visualizing and praying. I memorized the station I enjoyed so that every time I could listen to the same station. My goal was to keep my mind strong. So, that is what I listened to—positive and encouraging Christian and gospel music. It kept my mind focused on God, healing and hoping for the best. I did this for every appointment. I remember there were pictures on the ceiling so that the patients would have something to look at during their sessions.

Yes, I felt the burn. It was not quite like fire in the beginning. But eventually, as time went on, the heat in me increased. It's not like what you might think. The burn came from the side effects. Whenever I tried to use the bathroom, it was torture and I would have to go after every session of radiation. I knew that I was going to have to go to the bathroom as soon as I got off the table, so I would try to hold it until I made it back home, after my hour drive. Some days I would make it home. Other days, I barely made it to the bathroom down the hall at the hospital.

I thank God for my friend Taurus and his mother, Beverly. They talked to me throughout this process before treatment as Beverly's sister, Lynn, had previously gone through cervical cancer and the same exact treatment I was to experience. Lynn coached me and sent me healing affirmations, CDs and scriptures to help me get through. Beverly and Lynn helped to prepare me for the mental warfare I was bravely marching towards. Because of their advice, I knew I needed to listen to encouraging music while receiving radiation. Taurus visited me and was instrumental in being my personal nurse when I was home after surgery, which was a lifesaver for my mom and me. He was attentive towards me and displayed a true friendship. During times like this, having a great friend around helps with getting through each day. Even during treatment, he would often ask me to imagine that he was there with me as I got the *drip, drip, drip* and radiation, so I wouldn't feel alone.

My church family stepped in. Their acts of Christian love and kindness played such an important role in me maintaining my faith and it gave me strength and a new beginning. I felt so *empowered*. My church family at the time, Wingate United Methodist Church (WUMC), had a women's group called the Busy Group that made knitted prayer shawls. They would pray over them and present them to the sick. One Sunday during church service, they bestowed me with a prayer shawl. I felt that it symbolized the arms of God. These arms, I visualized, would hold me and keep me throughout the course of my cancer journey.

I wore that green knitted prayer shawl around my shoulders every single day. I wore it to and from my appointments. I only took it off to get radiation and as soon as I got off the table, I would put it back on. I slept with the prayer shawl because in my mind, when I wore it, God was with me. I came to learn later that this symbolism was an important part of my healing process. The covering was what kept my faith strong and my mind on pure thoughts.

I learned through the covering and prayers of others what God's Love—Agapé Love—really meant. I saw the expression of extravagant generosity at its best. This is what gave me *hope.* I was able to press on because of the generosity of countless men and women who came to my rescue when I was unable to care for myself.

I am often reminded of a time during my journey when Pastor Rhonda came to visit. It was like an angel from heaven had come to hear me and save me. As she checked to see how I was doing, she listened as I shared how my rides to and from the hospital were unbearable.

The assistance I received from a transportation service (that was supposed to be reliable) broke down every day to and from my appointments. Mind you, it was summertime and the sun, coupled with radiation, was no fun. It was quite draining. So, to be stranded daily, sometimes twice a day until the driver could get the car going or until someone came, was torturous for me as a radiation patient.

To my surprise, Pastor Rhonda set up a rotating schedule of drivers who were members from the church, who not only drove me to and from my appointments for a two hour round trip, but they sat with me throughout the entire process. I thought to myself, who are these people? I felt like they had just barely met me. I had been in North Carolina for only a year. Pastor Rhonda didn't stop there, she had a rotating schedule of families from the church to cook meals for my daughter, Kristyna Rose, and I.

Did I mention the church also helped me with my bills, as I was unable to work? Social service workers came to my house, since I was incapable of driving to them to fill out the paperwork for a small financial seed. My caseworkers, Patricia and Suzanne came and lifted my spirits with encouraging words as I filled out documents. I was amazed by their kindness. The little financial assistance I received from them to help me pay my bills, had been stolen from me the same day I cashed the check, and I didn't know how I was going to make it. WUMC stepped in, yet again. *But, God.*

My *hope* and *empowerment* continued as another cervical cancer patient provided me with relief. I met a beautiful young lady at my oncologist's office named Stacy. She was a few weeks ahead of me with receiving the same treatment for cervical cancer. She said she felt compassion when she learned that I was a single mother going through this journey practically alone. She couldn't imagine how I was making it, when she had her husband for support and it was still tough for her.

Stacy's husband, Scott, and son, Gavin, would come by and pick up Kristyna Rose and take her out to do various activities so that I could rest. Anyone that has had these treatments can understand how weak and tiring it is just to take care of yourself. There were times I couldn't give my two-year-old a bath, as it was painful to kneel, let alone walk anywhere. This family was like an answer to my prayers. God granted me grace, showing me that I had *something to live for.*

I felt a strong urge to bless others who were going through cancer because of the love I received from these good Samaritans who treated me so well, not even knowing me at all. I never wanted anyone else to experience what I had during my cancer journey. I felt my vision increase and my purpose in life take a shift.

Chapter 5

"We need to be angels for each other, to give each other strength and consolation. Because only when we fully realize that the cup of life is not only a cup of sorrow, but also a cup of joy, will we be able to drink it." – Henri Nouwen

The side effects of chemotherapy, boy, were they horrible. We are talking about severe nausea and vomiting. To fight these side effects, I was prescribed three different nausea medicines. I didn't always take them, as I was never fond of taking medicine. With me, taking the *drip, drip, drip*, I didn't want a whole lot of other chemicals in my body, too. So, I would endure a lot of it. I would only take the medicine if I couldn't bare it. When I did take it, sometimes I couldn't feel it working or I felt more miserable.

One remembrance that I can now laugh about regarding nausea was when my two-year-old would imitate me. She would go in the bathroom, pull up the toilet seat, lean her head into the toilet bowl, and pretend to vomit. She didn't quite understand and I presume thought it was normal behavior. Needless to say, I had to explain it to her and stop her at once.

Other side effects I endured from the chemotherapy were diarrhea and the loss in my ability to taste food. It was like I always had a metallic taste in my mouth. When I found something I could tolerate, I would try to gobble it down as fast as I could. This was because as soon as I took several bites, I would then get sick to my stomach. I remember going to a neighborhood cookout with my mom where her neighbor, Mr. Bill, had made some baked beans. I was super excited because I was nearly able to eat my entire bowl of them. I don't know what he had in those beans, but it worked.

The radiation seemed to kick my butt even more, which was agonizing pain. Another side effect I had from the radiation was fatigue. It also gave me an upset stomach almost immediately after, causing me to have diarrhea, nausea and vomiting. My skin would also get really sore, peel and it became darker. I think the part of radiation that impacted me the most was the internal radiation.

These brachytherapy treatments, also known as intracavitary brachytherapy, were experiences I would never want to see anyone else go through. I would have to go into surgery, they would put me to sleep, pack my vagina with cotton to protect my organs, then insert a metal device called a tandem, along with a small round holder called an ovoid. The tandem and ovoid treatment is when the radiation source is placed inside the body to conduct an internal radiation. Once the surgery was completed, I would be checked by way of a scan, to ensure everything was lined up correctly. Afterwards, I would have beads of radiation sent through the tandem and ovoid up my cervix. They would remove the device and I would then go home. I had five of these treatments at the tail end, no pun intended.

I was so glad when these sessions were over, as this was a painful process. Also, my time in the bathroom was unpleasant. As treatments progressed collectively, so did my pain. Hemorrhoids and diarrhea just don't go well together. It was to the point where I was ready to give up and go home to be with my Lord and Savior. It hurt to urinate and I was constantly nauseous. I didn't want to go any further.

What kept me was the constant *affirmation* of God's Word, prayers and healing. I spoke His Word over my mind and body. It was not easy, but I truly believed that's what did it for me. I coupled that with healing Bible verses of affirmations every day. I also visualized God healing my body. Whenever I drank water, I visualized taking communion.

In the Bible, it says that when we take communion, to do it in remembrance of Jesus (1 Corinthians 11:24; Luke 22:19). I did that with every drop of water I drank. I remembered Him and His blood that was shed for me. I declared that every drop was His blood healing me and purifying my body. I even remember saying to my radiation oncologist that the cancer was going to shrink so fast that his head was going to spin. It did shrink faster than what was normal, I was told at one of my appointments for internal radiation. So, they had to make some adjustments before my treatment. I believed it was truly God answering my prayers.

I remember someone suggesting to my mom and stepdad to take me to Bishop Tucker's church for prayer. His church was located on Walkup Avenue in Monroe, North Carolina. I will keep this memory in my mind forever. This church experience was a part of my healing process. I can't remember if it was a revival or a prayer service, however, when I walked in, weak and struggling to take steps, they immediately showed God's love through their compassion. Sitting was just as torturous as it was to stand, so they found a cushioned chair for me.

I remember a woman praying for me. She held her hand to my abdomen and prayed and prayed. I joined in, as I believe you should never have someone praying over you and you not pray for yourself. It was not always easy to pray, sometimes all I could say was, "Jesus." Thank God for intercessors like this lady who could pray for me when my prayers for myself felt weak.

At some point through the service, as everyone was praying, they did a faith walk. The lady stood me up and walked me back and forth across this long space where others were walking and praying. I can't even tell you who was there or how many people were in the room. I was focused only on my healing and God. I questioned God, wondering if the cancer was shrinking.

My confidence in my healing increased after this experience. I have never seen these people again. Ever. I pray this book gets into their hands, so they know how grateful I am for their obedience.

I pray that these great Samaritans, all of the pastors and churches, their faithful members, and that woman who prayed for me, receive bountifully from God for their obedience because I truly felt their love, compassion, extravagant generosity and prayers. They were pieces to a larger puzzle that contributed to my healing.

Chapter 6

"Healing may not be so much about getting better, as about letting go of everything that isn't you—all of the expectations, all of the beliefs—and becoming who you are."
– *Rachel Naomi Remen*

Life after cancer is not something that I heard discussed a lot once diagnosed with cancer. The process of treatment, and how you would overcome, was mostly in every conversation. As I headed back to work after my treatment was over, a subject that was not at the top of discussion with others, I had to adjust to my new life with my new body.

My new body was all too foreign, and I earnestly waited for us to reacquaint with each other. It's like a rebirth. So, for people who don't understand cancer-versaries, the celebration of life each year after being diagnosed and why they are so important, there is one reason. We experience a rebirth—life from new eyes—a new perspective—new understandings.

Life after cancer can be quite complicated and overwhelming. Survivor's remorse and posttraumatic stress disorder (PTSD) is not something you would quite naturally think about, but it is so real. I learned that a fellow survivor, Mrs. Covington, who I had chemo treatments with, had gotten sicker. Ironically, I worked with her daughter, La'Toya. Mrs. Covington had a smile that would turn any frown upside down and would sit and joke with me, talking for hours while we took the *drip, drip, drip*. When I learned that she had taken a turn for the worse, my family and I visited her and her family often. It was interesting that the pain of treatment was quite similar to what she described to me in her last days. I could relate all too well.

I held her hand and we would sing gospel songs and hymns. She sang so beautifully. Then, as life began to leave her, she would smile and squeeze my hand as I talked to her. She was too weak at times to speak. It hurt my soul because it was like I could feel her pain. It brought flashbacks to my own weakness and pain I experienced during my treatment. She had such a beautiful spirit about life and transitioning to go home to be with God. My last time seeing her, I made a promise that I would honor her.

When she transitioned to her now resting place, I experienced a mixture of emotions and survivor's remorse was one of them. I asked God why He spared my life and why she had to go. What could we have done differently? Her death hurt so badly. I don't know which was worse, seeing her suffer or seeing her go.

Or, was the thought of knowing I would still be here making it hurt even worse. Mrs. Covington and I had a special bond, which in her passing pushed me further towards my purpose. I wanted to honor her and other survivors. She inspired me as I moved on to be a new version of myself. This was a piece of the puzzle that contributed to my *transformation.*

After July 2009, a year later, I had been deemed cancer free. However, life after cancer was scary sometimes. After facing cancer, the awareness to my body heightened. I bled from my urethra about a year after I completed treatment. I saw blood every time I urinated. It was also painful. I was frightened that the cancer had returned. When I went to an urologist, the fear expanded. He gave me some pills that were to help with the pain I was having with urination and said that due to the radiation treatment, I probably would bleed for life. Can you imagine the trauma and stress I felt? I rebuked the thought of me bleeding for life, and thankfully I never went back to him again. The bleeding stopped about two months later and now, nine years later, still no blood.

Another time, I was frightened when I went to Urgent Care due to bleeding from my vagina. I was completely in menopause, so quite naturally, seeing blood alarmed me. The doctor told me that I should check with my oncologist because it looked like I still had cancer on my cervix. I called my nurse, frantic. She said it was the scar tissue that had developed on my cervix from the radiation. The problem here is that we still have doctors who are not familiar with what they see as it relates to cervical cancer and its treatment. That's why you must get more than one opinion when you want certainty and clarity.

As a result of my medical experiences, I didn't want just any kind of opinion. See, these doctors are not completely at fault. They don't specialize in gynecologic cancers. So, when I had a question, I learned from these experiences that I must question my oncologist and the nurses and not general practitioners or random doctors.

The fear of cancer returning is quite common for a survivor. It is natural since there is a risk for some cancers to return within five years of treatment. So, five years in I still had questions and doubts with every little thing that looked like a hint of cancer symptoms. I was even referred to an amazing physical therapist, Barbara. As she gave me vaginal and rectal therapy to help with the side effects of the radiation, she taught me about the pelvic floor, its relationship to the vagina, and how it operates. The therapy sometimes caused me to bleed because the tissue is thin and sensitive. Again, I thought the cancer had returned on several occasions during physical therapy.

The stressful experience of having changes to the vagina, can be traumatic during treatment, but can be a roller coaster ride, after treatment. If a cancer patient does not take the steps to heal mentally, spiritually and emotionally, the physical issues will feel magnified. However, the trauma of trying to face physical therapy, the results of how my body changed, the fact that at 28, I entered into menopause and could no longer have children and that I had hot flashes and mood swings was overwhelming. This is, in short, what some survivors go through. Life after cancer is what I wished someone had talked me through. The best part about it is that I have made it through, to share with you, how you can too.

Chapter 7

"Perhaps, we should love ourselves so fiercely, that when others see us, they know exactly how it should be done." – Rudy Francisco

This experience has taught me many things and one of them is how to love myself. I became celibate in 2010 and committed my body back to God. It's not so bad most days, but I almost gave in once when I lowered my standards.

Loving yourself requires you to stand firm to your standards. Stand your ground on what you believe despite how you feel at any given moment. I learned to love myself, and all my quirky ways. I learned that I needed to push beyond how I felt about my past, so I could move forward into my future. I learned that I could forgive myself for having cancer. Yes, I blamed myself. I learned that it's okay to mess up and try again. I learned to look in the mirror and love what I see.

Regardless of what the world felt about me, I learned I had the power to create and invent the life that I wanted and how I saw it to be. I learned that the opinion of other people was not who I was, but that I had the power to be bold and courageous, creative and dynamite. I have learned not to give up on me because of faults and failures that sometimes consume me.

For me, life after cancer encompasses all of the H. E.A.T.—Hope, Empowerment, Affirmation and Transformation. I've lived that out ever since I fought to ring the bell. Ringing the bell symbolizes the end of treatment. For me, the bell symbolizes when my life truly began. My new birth. So, I celebrate two births, one in February, my natural birth, and another in July, my God-given rebirth when my cancer treatment ended.

I began the transformation to be the amazing woman that I knew I was created to be—the woman that was sent to walk into my divine destiny. People who know me have only been introduced to the old me—the soft spoken, timid, shy, doubtful, not trusting myself, me. The me that was a doormat to the word yes. I have since learned to step over the doormat and open the door with the word no. I had to learn that some of life's best opportunities only come from saying NO.

Loving myself taught me about having self-worth. A thread that carried throughout my life and my being was doing everything for everyone. I gave of myself to others and neglected to do what was most important for me. I learned to care more for me—to pay attention to my needs and not be bound solely by the needs of others.

I searched for my strengths, and as I did, God sent messengers who would call on my greatness. The new me unfolded. The calling for me to work with single mothers, cancer survivors and business owners was birthed. When the hurt and pains of life healed, and I shared my story more and more, I saw that there were others who needed not only my story, but my pains, sorrows and fears. They needed to see that they were not alone and that there was a way out and a way through.

As time progressed, the vision of myself that God showed me, unfolded. I encountered strong and em-powered women who also had amazing stories. These women showed up in different areas of my life. Some were going through their breakthrough and walked alongside me as we discovered our way. Others had already gone through and now shared how they managed to make it on the other side, to their freedom. It is through these newfound relationships that I learned the importance of positive relationships and com-munication. Connecting with like-minded individuals, while also sharing positive thoughts and life experiences, was beneficial to the growth of my personal and professional development.

On my walk through to my transformation, I had to work on being self-empowered and self-motivated. Being self-empowered takes work. It's a process that many forfeit because of the parts of their personality that they must work at overcoming. The parts of you that you love and that you hate. The parts that make you squirm and the parts you really want to keep to yourself. However, those are the parts you must find a true confidant or mentor to help you through. Keeping secrets of your personal weaknesses will only keep you bound. It is when you face these challenging areas that you can be set free and delivered from them.

Self-motivation is another area that is a sore spot. It is a skill that some are born with and some who must work at it. I learned that I must motivate myself to get out of a slump because that was how I would see real change. No one would be able to convince me or motivate me out of my pit like I could. Again, this skill is one that requires time to acquire if it is not something that is already practiced.

I never really thought about these skills as something I would one day need to concentrate on. I went to school, graduated, got a job and that was all I was taught as the major things I needed to focus on in life. I have now learned that school is not enough. Getting a job is not enough. Life is so much more fulfilling when it has purpose.

Once I connected with my purpose, my life took major turns. I learned that depression and anxiety cannot thrive in a purpose-lived life. Joy and peace are welcomed more gracefully in a life that is open to possibilities. Doubt and unbelief drowned me and kept me from moving ahead.

I like to call anxiety and depression the Bonnie and Clyde syndrome. See, these two were seen together doing their crimes, stealing and taking things that were not theirs. And these two would kill anyone that got in their way during the Great Depression. The name is something I came up with because depression and anxiety steals your joy, energy and all signs of life. Depression and anxiety not only takes from you physically, but they drain you spiritually, emotionally and socially. They kill every dream and desire you ever had of doing anything great in your life.

Here we have two culprits causing you to remain inward and away from the rest of the world. How can you ever accomplish anything great alone? You can't. You need others. A life filled with purpose will cause you to attack and defeat anxiety and depression. You must work at this daily if this struggle is the norm for you.

Setting goals and working toward them helped me. Being mindful of who I had in my ear helped me. Speaking life over myself—mind, body and soul— helped me. Speaking over my home, family, goals and future helped me.

I literally have had to drag myself out of a pit that no one on earth could help me do. I learned all of the tactics, strategies and how to pray from other people. However, the work had to be done by me and me alone. Prayer helped, but God couldn't get me out of my mess. I had to do the work. God sent me certain people to give me what I needed, and then I had to take the steps, risks and overcome my own stinking thinking in order to pull myself through. I knew I had to do it. Not only for my own wellbeing, but also for my daughter, my family, and those millions of lives I would touch by doing so.

PART II:

A JOURNEY

THROUGH JOURNALING

The Enemy in Me

I used to love writing when I was in high school, especially in my junior and senior years. One of my teachers said, "Excelsior, excelsior. Onward and upward." This is what I have strived for even when I didn't know how. I searched for answers on how to keep going forward.

Those days and nights when I woke up, trying to pull my hair out because life just didn't seem to be going my way. I wanted to write about my frustrations, but I just couldn't muster the words to put on paper. In 2012, for my birthday, a young lady placed a journal in my hands and told me, "Begin writing and it will get easier and easier."

It took me awhile to start writing again because of fear. My heart raced and my hands could not move as fast as thoughts were coming to me. However, I tried. One day I sat down and began, the words would not stop. I was so shocked. What had happened to me? *Words are my friend*, I thought.

I reflected back when I was a little girl and loved words just as Maya Angelou had spoken about when she was young. When I read her story, I thought, *Yes, me too.* I loved the way words made me feel when I said them, when I wrote them and when I read them. I loved to read the words that made up books and poems—the words that were penned in the Bible that stirred my spirit every time I parted it open. The words my teachers would speak that were challenging to others only delighted me. Yes, sometimes even secretly, I would think of how awesome the teacher was as he or she read books that put my peers to sleep. My only problem was staying focused long enough to get through it all. My heart now chuckles at the thought of it all. So, you get my drift? The point is that my love for words and writing finally returned and it all started with the discovery of *The Enemy in Me*.

When I started to write this, I thought about how it had been for me—my mindset. It was the hold up from me getting to my greatness. I was the reason that I had not been bold and courageous to get past life after cancer. It had been me that slowed down my process of experiencing the freedom I felt I needed and deserved. It's typically the enemy in me versus the enemy of the world outside of me. For 20 years, I created my own mental sabotage that ran like a broken record in my head. The art of writing was the key that I needed to unlock and overcome this enemy within me.

The Enemy In Me

I prayed
Oh Lord, You are the architect
I don't understand
I don't know Your plan
Lord, take my hand
Wrap me in Your arms and hold me tight.

I prayed
Oh Lord, I don't understand
How could this be?
How did this happen
How did this happen to me?

I'm at a place from time to time
Where tears just won't fall
I prayed and wore my prayer shawl
Keeping visions of God
In my head, on my mind
Each and every time I thought about—
Every time I felt—
Every time—
death
lurked across my cerebellum.

"Not now," I cried
I yelled, "Not now"
It feels so surreal
All I could think about is,
You couldn't possibly know how I feel.

You say, "It's going to be okay"
"You are healed"
Then, I would find strength
Somewhere—somehow—within
I then believed,
Okay—I will win.

But how?
How fast is it growing?
What's going on inside?
Is it traveling down the stream—
The stream of toxic blood
Through my veins
To my organs?
Is it really all in one place?
I wish I could see—
This haunting, lurking
Killer inside of me.

I was told that controlling your mind
Was half the battle
Being positive and
Keeping the faith
Would help to pull one through.

As I walked across the stage
As they prayed for me
Speaking life into me
I asked, "Lord, am I healed?
I trust You Lord
I know You can."

"God, it's hard to trust You
When I hear,

"What if it comes back?"
Voices from the world
Voices from within
The enemy in me
I cannot
Let—it—WIN.

Take a Moment and Reflect

What are some ways that you have allowed the enemy in you to overtake and prevent you from moving forward to be all that you were created to be?

_____

_____

_____

_____

What steps can you take to expand your mind to encourage and empower yourself?

_____

_____

_____

_____

_____

_____

Your Turn

Share your story on how you have been faced with self-debilitating thoughts. How has your mind kept you from moving forward? How have you overcome your mindset?

_____

_____

_____

_____

_____

_____

_____

_____

_____

_____

_____

_____

_____

Turn Your Self-Talk into Self-Love

The battlefield of the mind can be conquered when you overcome what you think of yourself. Your self-talk will reveal how you think about yourself. If someone heard what you said to yourself, about yourself, what would they learn about you? Will it line up with what you exhibit on the outside?

You have what it takes within you to change your self-talk, so it is positive. When you line up your self-talk with your purpose, magic happens. When you speak words of love and encouragement to yourself about yourself, everything around you will line up, too. If you think you're ugly, why would you expect anyone else to say anything different about you? If you feel that your lips are too big or too small, why get upset when someone else says those words to you? However, when you look in the mirror and learn to love what you see, so will the rest of the world. Your self-talk can empower or disempower you. Speaking down on your abilities and what you feel your potential is, attacks you in the same way and with the same intensity as someone else saying those words to you.

Self-love is major in the life filled with H. E. A. T. (Hope, Empowerment, Affirmation and Transformation). Before my cancer diagnosis, the view I had of myself was not a beautiful, sexy or smart view. By the time I was faced with cancer, I was torn down both internally and externally, mentally and spiritually. Then, I woke up and started working every day on getting better. I began speaking life back to myself through the repetition of empowering and encouraging words. I took time to believe in what was possible instead of the impossible. I studied the word *believe* and what it meant to my mind and body. Believing took on a new meaning. It was confirmed when I won a gift at a direct sales business event. The prize was a teal-colored sign that said, "Believe."

When I joined the direct sales company, Traci Lynn Fashion Jewelry, on October 16, 2010, it introduced me to strategies and skills, experts and dynamite men and women. I learned how to build relationships and friendships while offering customer service to my clients who loved the statement pieces and handbags that I sold. Building a team in this organization filled me with tons of learning opportunities such as organization, speaking, coaching, training, mentoring, time and money management, sales and leadership. I also learned how to build a business, party planning and presentation skills. It gave me what I needed to believe in me and to make the transition to La Luz.

La Luz means "The Light" in Spanish. La Luz is the name that God gave me during my most intimate moments of prayer with him. I am the light by the way I live my life. I am the light in how I speak and act. I shine light into dark places by being the best representation of God I can be.

My goal is to help people see how they can connect with their purpose for living while they develop and share their own stories, just as I have. I learned to stand my ground and face the battlefield in my mind. It was during this transformation that I saw major changes in my life, built on my strengths while forgiving my weaknesses.

One day after receiving radiation, I was being pushed in a wheelchair out of the hospital to my transportation when a beautiful woman passed me. My spirit spoke to me as she walked by. I thought to myself, *What does she see when she looks in the mirror?* At that time, I had lost so much weight that I was down to 115 pounds and could literally see my bones. Tears fell from my eyes as I reflected on the person I once was.

At this moment in time, looking in the mirror was painful. I thought to myself that I needed to write about how I felt so that I could reflect on my thoughts about myself at that time. I also felt it was something that I could share with others, so they knew that they were not alone. Changes to my body's interior were just part of the pain and suffering to my mindset. What I looked like on the outside contributed to this as well. So, what do you see? Here's a glimpse into what I saw when I looked at me.

Beautiful. Strong. Empowered.

When I look in the mirror
I don't know who I am.
I see pictures of myself and I ask,
"Who is she?"
How can we
Be one in the same?
Who is she?
Beautiful
Strong
Empowered.

My mind stays in the past so
I must pull it forward
Thinking of the queen I am
Beautiful inside and out
The bold me
The strong me
Covering ground that has never been seen.

Empowered to move mountains
That's been formed all around me
Mountains in my mind,
Mountains in my heart
Now, it's time for the mountains to part
Beautiful
Strong
Empowered.

My mirrored view
No longer distorted
I see clearly now
Clearer than ever

I am all that I see me to be
And more
I am Beautiful
I am Strong
I am Empowered.

What Do You See?

When you look in the mirror
What do you see?

I see death looking back at me
I see skin turning pale
I see weight falling off
I see hope looking back at me.

When I look in the mirror
I see eyes staring at me
I see needles sticking me
I see blankets wrapped around me
I see someone in need of
doctors, nurses, and technicians.
What do you see?

When I look in the mirror
I see bones with skin
Popping out like they're in 3D
I see fear trying to paralyze me
I see dreams past deferred
I see black and red marks to identify me.
What do you see?

In the mirror, there are many
That's whom I see
Many who have had cancer.
What do I see?

I see a survivor—a strong survivor
A survivor
That's ME.

Take a Moment and Reflect

What do you see when you look in the mirror?

_____

_____

_____

_____

_____

_____

The views you have of yourself will make or break your momentum to your greatness. What steps can you take to improve what you see?

_____

_____

_____

_____

_____

_____

_____

Your Turn

Share your story on how you feel when you look at yourself. How has the view of yourself kept you from moving forward?

_____

_____

_____

_____

_____

_____

_____

_____

_____

_____

_____

_____

_____

_____

_____

"God, grant me the serenity
To accept the things I cannot change;
Courage to change the things I can;
And wisdom to know the difference."

~ Reinhold Neibuhr

Serenity. Courage. Wisdom.

Serenity
Courage
Wisdom
Three words that gave me strength
The prayer that held me together
When I asked God why.

I can't change this, but
I can change that.
My mind. My life.
I do know the difference
The difference between
What has me and what I hold inside me.

Yes, there's a difference between
Knowing and believing
That cancer can't have you
Unless you let it.

In me, I have strength and power.
I hold it
I possess it
I own it
I have serenity, courage and wisdom power.

The mind is power
Power that is released when it is
Put to use
Power that conquers
Power that transforms
Power that heals.
I have—

Serenity
Courage
Wisdom
Power—
In me
Working through me like
The red and white blood cells
That flows through my veins.

I must take the time to
Use my bright mind
Use my imagination and vision
Use my creativity and enact my dreams
To action
To action that accepts life
While taking action to make life—
Exciting
Interesting
Full
Free and
Fun.

You know,
To make life—
Serene
Courageous
Wise
Three words that gave me strength
When I asked God... Why?

Take a Moment and Reflect

Self-talk can turn into self-love or self-hate. Words are powerful. The words you speak to yourself, about yourself, can build you up or break you down. If you struggle with positive self-talk, you are not alone. This written exercise will help you.

Think about areas of your life where you don't feel empowered. Write those areas down. It may be in your profession. It may be in your relationships. Which areas are you struggling with in life? Open up for your breakthrough, and let go.

○ _____

○ _____

○ _____

○ _____

○ _____

○ _____

○ _____

○ _____

What are the words that make you feel powerful and courageous to push through? You will want to use these words regularly. Place them around your home, use them in conversations and take time daily to find more words that you can use to strengthen your mindset. Use these words to empower you in the areas you listed above. (Ex. bold, confident, strong, fearless, beautiful, vibrant, etc.)

○ _____   ○ _____

○ _____   ○ _____

○ _____   ○ _____

○ _____   ○ _____

○ _____   ○ _____

○ _____   ○ _____

○ _____   ○ _____

Your Turn

Share your story about a time when you operated in 100% self-love. What do you do to maintain the love of self? If this is an area you need to strengthen, share how you want to feel about yourself from this moment forward if you could have the ideal love of self.

_____

_____

_____

_____

_____

_____

_____

_____

_____

_____

_____

_____

_____

Put on Your Crown, Diva

The thing that has broken you—the thing that has consumed you—the thing that has torn you down, flipped you around and shook your world until it crumbled into millions and billions of pieces—yes, that thing—it may be the thing that has made you stronger. Life experiences have created you to be the awesome person you have become. Embrace the brokenness. The moments you have grown to hate—learn to love them. It is what makes you fierce and unstoppable.

Look at it from a different perspective and life as you know it will be transformed. You have made it before, and you surely can, and will, do it again. Once you absorb this to be true, you will enjoy and love life in a way that will blow your mind. People will look at you in amazement when they hear your story. After knowing what you have been through, they won't be able to fathom how you made it. They will wonder how you kept going.

It is your purpose birthed from your pain that keeps you moving. It's your destiny that is discovered through your dirt—your divine destiny. So, as a child of the Most High, put on your crown, Diva and walk into your divine destiny.

Own It

Choose
I choose to own it
Own me
Own my right to be me,
To be free.

I own it—ALL
My dreams and goals,
My child and my home
I own my healing
In my mind, healing in my soul
Emotional stability that only I can control.

When I was young, walking the catwalk,
I thought, *she couldn't be me*
I stepped off the platform
And then I would retreat
Low Self-esteem
No Confidence.

I gave up on everything
Then, one day, I woke up
With tough accountability
I see it now
It's running deep down in me
I can strut on stage and off
Hold my head up high
Becoming one with Naomi
La Luz, The Light.

Shoulders round, feet solid on the ground
I own me—the me I never thought I could be

Remember when you asked me,
Why I could not be the same person I was on stage?
Didn't you major in theatre?
I used to believe *that's—just—not—me*
Now I know I can transform into anything.

You used to call me Minnie Mouse
Because of my soft, soft, timid voice
Now they call me the motivator,
Who's moving and shaking, changing lives.
I own her
The ME I used to hide.
I'd walk off the stage and thought I had to fly
Fly—fly away to another place
Because if I stayed here, I'd have to face HER
You know her
The one who stands up for herself
Who looks at others and realize that she's just as—
AMAZING
STRONG
BEAUTIFUL and
AWESOME

You know her
The one who looks at cancer and says—
You don't OWN ME
NOW, GO TO HELL
The one who stands up when she
Really wants to sit down
The one who's living the life SHE desires
Yeah, she's owning it
That's what they say when they realize
She wasn't always that way.
I speak of voices from the world,

The voices within
Transforming the thoughts that once had me
Locked in
Trapped in my mind
Keeping me bound
I wouldn't move forward,
Shoot, I could hardly make a sound
But then, one day—
I snapped out of that trance
I'm now so free and jolly.

I own my world my way
From now on, Naomi is here to stay
So, watch out world,
It's my time to shine
No holding me back now
I'm owning everything from A to Z
So, if you're with me,
And owning your destiny,
SHOUT with me—
I—AM—ME.

Hey, Martinez. Hey, Morales.
I know What It's Like.

I know what it's like
To look in the mirror and not like
What I see
I know what it's like
To feel ugly and raggedy
I know what it's like
To feel little and blue
Someone once said
To love and cherish what's
Inside of you.

It may seem bleak and like a dream
To give yourself love and
Offer YOU everything
No one knows just what you need
So guess what, my dear queen
You are the dream.

Start with one word
Or maybe even two
Speak to yourself
As a person all anew.
It comes a time
When life will go away
Why not start now
Why not have your own parade?
Now is your time
To just let it flow
Open your mouth, mind—and—let go.

This is the season
That some will never see
I know. I get it.
You ask, "Why me?"
You have what it takes within you to be
All of the most glorious things
You could even imagine being.

So, please, take time to say
I—Love—You—
Not to your friend, family, mother, or boo
Yes, say I—love—you—
Not to your father, husband, or children you see
Now is your time to say,
I—Love—ME.

Take a Moment and Reflect

There are times in life when society, family and friends feel compelled to tell you what to do and how to do it. There are times when they try to define who you are. When words are spoken to you by others about who they feel you are long enough, it is easy to conform and agree. On the other hand, you might be dreaming of a new you—a different you. That's okay. Embrace this version of yourself. Let's expose your authentic self and reveal to the world who you really are. You must recognize this negative chatter that you are saying to yourself or that others have said about you. You can't fix what you haven't taken time to recognize. Take a moment and identify the person you are NOT?

_____

_____

_____

_____

_____

_____

_____

_____

_____

_____

_____

_____

_____

_____

_____

_____

_____

_____

_____

_____

_____

_____

_____

_____

_____

Your Turn

You are a diva created for greatness. You were created to achieve amazing things. There are people who you were born to bless. But, not being your authentic self, you can't possibly walk in the complete authority you were created for. So, take a moment right now to write out who YOU ARE, not who you pretend to be. Write out who YOU KNOW YOU ARE, not who you were told you WERE.

_____

_____

_____

_____

_____

_____

_____

_____

_____

_____

_____

_____

_____

_____

_____

_____

_____

_____

_____

_____

_____

_____

_____

_____

_____

_____

_____

A Family's Legacy

Although cancer is not a person, it speaks LOUDLY to people that have come face to face with it. To date, cancer has no cure that we know of and has claimed the lives of countless families. This fact speaks volumes. It's loud and annoying. I want it to shut up as well as many others who have walked in my shoes. Some of those people are family members who I hold near and dear to my heart.

I don't like to give power to the word cancer so often times I call it little c, as not to make it bigger than my faith, nor my belief in the power of healing. I have written about my family's connection with little c and my frustration with the fact that they were impacted or have even died because of it. I have had to deal with my cancer diagnosis as well as face the news of family members receiving a diagnosis. Some are still alive today to share their story. Others have passed away, leaving behind their legacy. Next, I share some of my thoughts regarding family members who have seen the face of cancer.

Cancer Speaks

Cancer speaks
It creeps in quietly and slowly
It tears down a healthy home
Cancer yells
It is territory bound
It wants it all
Cancer whispers
It steals
It trespasses
Cancer twirls
Cancer kills
Cancer—I HATE CANCER
Live on, Keesha La Luz Carter
Live on, Aunt Evelyn Belford
Live on, Sister Trina Baker
Live on, Cousin Lorraine Walker
Live on, Cousin Sakinah Salahu-Din
Live on, Cousin Izetta Dunn
Live on, Cousin Jacqualyn Murphy-Wells
Rest on, Grandma Vester Carter
Rest on, Daddy Lenard George Washington Carter
Rest on, Uncle Arthur Carter
Rest on, Cousin Andre Dubose
Rest on, Aunt Betty Dubose
Rest on, Uncle James (Jack) Dunn
Rest on, Uncle Barry Williams
I hate cancer
I hate cancer
I hate cancer
I hate cancer
You shall rest on
We shall live on.

I'm a Carter

I'm a Carter
I'm a fighter
It's deep down in the roots
It's deep down in my blood
Thank you, God
I'm taking over where my ancestors left off
They left clues
They left footprints
Strength they displayed through their lives
Continues to pull me together
I'm thankful because I can hold
The strengthened strings they have
Left behind.
The places they could not pull through
The roads they could not travel
I'm moving on to capture the dream
They once hoped to live.

Your Turn

Do you have your family history in writing regarding the little c? If not, write their names and relationship to you below. Make a list and check it twice. You may see patterns from the past that can help protect your future. Ask questions when you visit the doctor about what you can learn from your family's cancer history. It's your body. It's your life. Advocate for your health.

Circle M=Maternal or P=Paternal. Continue on another sheet of paper for more space.

Family Member _____

Relationship _____ M/P

Family Member _____

Relationship _____ M/P

Family Member _____

Relationship _____ M/P

Family Member _____

Relationship _____ M/P

Family Member _____

Relationship _____ M/P

Family Member _____

Relationship _____ M/P

Family Member _____

Relationship _____ M/P

Family Member _____

Relationship _____ M/P

Family Member _____

Relationship _____ M/P

Family Member _____

Relationship _____ M/P

Family Member _____

Relationship _____ M/P

Family Member _____

Relationship _____ M/P

Family Member _____

Relationship _____ M/P

Family Member _____

Relationship _____ M/P

Family Member _____

Relationship _____ M/P

Family Member _____

Relationship _____ M/P

Family Member _____

Relationship _____ M/P

Taking Action

One day, I learned that my life would never level out as long as I laid in bed pouting, wishing things to be different. There was no way, or no how I was ever going to get my life together doing the things I had already done again and again. I learned that this is the definition of insanity, expecting things to change when I had made no changes.

The cure for this was for me to take action. Not just a little action, but massive action. As I moved forward to transform my life, everything around me changed. I dressed differently. I spoke differently. I stood differently. I even cut off my hair. My habits changed and my passions and desire for greatness in my life increased to levels that they had never done before. Life was fulfilling for me in a way that was more than just a fly-by kind of thing. I enjoyed life daily.

The Bonnie and Clyde Syndrome disappeared with no more depression and anxiety. Well, anxiety came, but not like before. I was able to wipe away depression completely. When it tried to poke out its sneaky face, I would move ferociously to a goal and it would disappear again. I figured it out, finally.

The secret to overcoming the worst moments in my life, and the tormenting feelings of depression and anxiety, was for me to take massive actions. So, here I talk about what it was like for me when I did.

Taking Action

Enduring birth pains to gain the new me
Taking A.C.T.I.O.N.
Acting on action
Creatively and courageously
Trusting God
In spite of me and my circumstances
Over and over to the
New me—New time—New life

I'm going to get my blessings
They're mine
You can't have them
Give them back to me
I'm taking action and
Moving forward
One stop and one move at a time
I'm taking action and
moving forward,
knocking down one door at a time.
I'm taking action and
Moving forward
To the New me
It's My time
It's My life.

Ringing Out

"Ring this bell,
Three times well
It's toll to clearly say
My treatment's done
This course is run
And I am on my way."
~Unknown

The "Ringing Out" poem may be found next to a bell hanging on a wall in the infusion or radiation office. Ringing out, a symbol of completion for a cancer survivor, let's everyone know that he or she is ringing out of treatment. It's a moment to celebrate. The time to rejoice. Others that are standing around typically celebrate with you. Some survivors have friends and family to join them for this wonderous occasion, just to see them "Ring Out."

I thought I was going to miss my opportunity to ring the bell. I mentioned to my nurse that my last internal radiation treatment was in the basement, where there was not a bell hanging on the wall. All of my chemotherapy and radiation treatments were complete and I wanted to go through the ritual of "Ringing Out." As you could imagine, I was excited when I could finally say, "It's MY day to ring."

It's MY Day to Ring

I open my eyes as the sunrays shine brightly on my face
Tick tock
The clock is racing
Tick tock
What's happening?
My face is pale
I am weak

The door opens
I can hardly lift my feet
Yellow shirt brings the chair
I slowly slide out and
Plop
Plop
Plop

I am finally there
My butt lands in the wheelchair
Hello
Hello
I'm so glad you're here
Your hair, it's still there
Flowing black and strong
Your smile... how do you bear?
It's
It's
It's
My mind
Yes, that's it

It's cold
Burr, burr, burr

I tightly wrap my prayer shawl
Around
And around and around
It goes—to comfort me
And give me strength
The hand of God
The love I know
It's pure and clear
No
One
Can
See
Him
But, He speaks
LOUDLY
And
s o f t l y.

We are
Rolling
Rolling
Rolling
Down the long stretch
I stretch
Stretch
Stretch
Up three floors to the infusion room
7 A.M. to 4 P.M.
I take poison into my blood
That's what I called it
The drip
Drip
Drip
That makes me sick

Weak
Thin
The heat from the machine that turns
Turns
Turns
Around my belly
Side
Butt
Side
And back around again
Machines and needles now become my friend
A vulnerability that can only be given
When all of me is exposed to people I
Do
Not
Know
A vulnerability that can only be given
By that thing called c
An
Cer
Can answer
Can you answer
ME?
A vulnerability that can only be given
But takin'
my spirit
My heart
My identity.

My love
Love
Love has dried up
As a raisin in the sun
Dream passed deferred

I cry, but why?
I think
The Lord's on my side.

Almost done
Surgery
Again
Here we go
Again
Surgery
Again
I remember the first one was when
We learned it had spread to my
Lymph nodes and moved me from
II b to III
So, here we go
Again
Surgery
Again
To pack my vagina in
To protect the walls from the hot
Heat
That burns from within
Small beads that they shoot in
Meeeeeeeee.

I feel isolated and so not freeeeee
As they hide behind the wall and count
1, 2, 3
The metal rod hangs out of me
That's attached to me
It hurts but I endure as the morphine is all I can stand
That drips in my hand
I look to the right and I think again

As they hide behind the wall and count
1, 2, 3
Why hide and leave
ME?
I know, I know
It's to slowly kill the fast growing monster that's in me
It's quick and it's over
Bang
Bang
Bang
The beads of heat go up into
The vaginal cavity
They live there to conquer the monster
Fi-na-lly.

They shrink so fast your head
Spins
Spins
Spins
Finally, it's the end
Ding
Ding
Ding.

You almost forgot
It's MY day to ring
Ring
Ring
The bell of The End.

The end?
The end
But not really
'Cause

Now, I see, this
Is
Just
The beginning.

Letters to Little c

I Am Who I Am Because Of YOU

I am who I am because of YOU
Thank you, little c, for pushing
Me to my greatness
Thank you for helping me to peel
Back those layers of reality
That had previously been buried.

A reality that exposes the
Truth in me.
Fearless, Bold, and
Courageous
What was meant
For my bad has ultimately been
Turned around for my greatness

Yes, and AMEN
Greatness has
Emerged for a new level and
Dimension of life that was
A long-kept secret
No longer
Lied to,
I embrace my—
Truth.

I Hear You Calling Me

I hear you calling me loud and clear
I don't want to listen to you
You are speaking a language that I despise
A language that makes me SICK.

I am keeping my ears open to life, healing and joy
STOP YELLING
Your voice means nothing to me
You're asking me why I am yelling at you?
Because YOU HURT ME.

Am I to be numb?
Am I supposed to act like you don't exist?
Am I to act like I don't care that you abused me?
Violated me? HUH?
You took my inner most being and
Tried to make it yours.
Sorry baby, but you don't live here anymore.

Take a Moment and Reflect

How do you feel about cancer? Have you thought about cancer as if it were a person before? If you could talk to little c, what would you say?

_____

_____

_____

_____

_____

_____

_____

_____

_____

_____

_____

_____

_____

_____

Your Turn

If you have ever been in a position where you can't take care of yourself, home or children due to your health, you can imagine how it feels to have been hit by cancer. If you received help from friends, family or even strangers, I'm sure there are thoughts or words that you would want to share with them. Here is your moment.

_____

_____

_____

_____

_____

_____

_____

_____

_____

_____

_____

_____

I'm a Teal Diva

The moment I connected with Shannon Routh, I knew we were destined to have an amazing friendship. What I did not know was how we would connect through our nonprofit organizations that support other cancer survivors. Her organization, Teal Diva, hosts various fundraisers throughout the year where she, in turn, gives back to cancer research, provides awareness in the community, and most of all, support survivors through events and an exclusive gynecologic cancer survivor retreat.

It is through her pushing me to my greatness to do what I love, that I have blossomed and become more daring to reach my goals. I have had the honor and privilege to conduct journaling workshops. She gave me my first opportunity to do so at her very first survivor retreat. Neither of us was sure how it would turn out, however she loved it and has asked me to return ever since.

From these workshops, I gained confidence and continued to develop my content and format. I have since had the blessed opportunity to present at other retreats and workshops, such as the Fighting Cancer, Inc.'s Christian Survivor Retreat and a workshop held and sponsored by the Novant Health Buddy Kemp Cancer Support Center in Charlotte, North Carolina. It gives me so much joy to work with these women and survivors that I always find time to write something of my own each time I present. Some of the journal passages in this book have come from these workshops and are as therapeutic for me as I pray they are for all who attend.

Teal Diva

I've fantasized about a day when I…
Don't have to think about YOU
A day when I'm not giving you too much credit
You, taking me places I never wanted to go
Wandering in a state of hypnosis,
Unaware of what was next or
What was happening to me.

Lost in a world where I feel alone
But, have a sea of love poured out over me
My eyes can't see it all because
You have me in a trance.

I woke up one day and my world was
Turned upside down.
Within three seconds, three words were spoken
That would erase my worldview
You—have—cancer.
REALLY? Are you kidding me?

I've fantasized about a day when I…
Can look in the mirror and see a woman
Who's confidently in love with love again
A day when I don't remember the men and women
Putting their hands in my vagina…
Stretching me… *IT HURTS*
Looking at me… examining me…
Sticking me with needles… asking ME to relax
RELAX? YOU RELAX.

There's no part of me that wants to relax
I didn't ask to be here

Blood—bowels—and bare-bodied
Bs that I was forced into by YOU
Come on now—You can't tell me you are not sneaky
Creeping up on me when I was
Trying to fulfill my dreams.

Dreams. Dreams. Dreams.

I wake up to my reality. A fantasy
That I'll have until the day I go home
Where I'm physically no longer here
But spiritually, I'll continue to live on—
Live on in the fight—inspiring, encouraging,
And empowering others through my legacy
Until then—
I'll reign free to be me
A queen and Teal Diva that's now moving on
To fantasize a day when you will be NO MORE.

Teal Diva Retreat—Workshop #1

The first day I met you,
I never knew you were
Going to change my life
Forever. I didn't know what
To expect, really. You knew
A lot about me—Ha—and me
I knew very little about you.

The first day I met you,
My mind raced to figure
Out the depths and heights
Of the impact you were
Making on me

Restless nights
Hot flashes
Blood from the front and
The back
Nausea
Prayer shawl
Praying
Doctor visits nearly everyday
Wondering if I'll be with
My daughter on graduation
And wedding day

You pushed yourself onto me
What did you expect?
I know you didn't think I
Was going to just let
You come into my life
And treat me any kind

Of way. Ahh, you took
My femininity
You raped
Me mentally, physically
And emotionally.
Huh? Really? I'm supposed
To let you in? How can I,
Little c?

Wake up
Wake up
Before you go—wait
I need to tell you something
Uh uh, don't you do it
Before they give you another drop
Of poison
Before you die
Listen up
This is MY body
You can't have it
This is MY soul
You can't have it
You took the most intimate
Parts of me and violated me.
You took my femininity and you
Thought it was okay
WAIT
WAIT
Don't you go to sleep
Until I tell you to, I am
Going to be aggressive with YOU,
Just as you violated ME
I'm taking it ALL back
YES.

I was living five years with the
Pain, insecurities, fear, doubts,
And riding random emotional roller coasters
NO MORE
I'm taking
My body BACK
I shall live
And not die
YOU, however,
DIE
Go to sleep.

Even though you have left my body
And have shown no signs
For nine years—you left me
Behind with scars.
Scars that can't be seen with the
Naked eye. Scars that
Walk with me physically.
The scars on my belly. The
Scars inside my vaginal
Walls and on my cervix's
Surface. The scars on my
Intestines, colon, and urethra.
YES. You knew what you were doing
Time is up
On you lingering on. You
Will no longer keep me in
Mental bondage. I take
Control over my mind,
My memory. Yes, I AM
Free and liberated from
Feeling abandoned, worthless
And abused. YOU RAPED

ME. You tortured me. You
Took what I thought was
The one thing no one
Could ever take from me
In this way. I've woken
Up to reality. I realize
That you are a serial
Rapist and serial killer.

So, as I put you away
From my interior cerebellum
And take back my life,
I am going to continue to
FIGHT
 I know you have
An army of friends
And allies—but
That won't
Stop me
That won't
Keep me away
Although,
You have left me—
I'm going to fight for other
Survivors. I'm going to
Run to their aid. We
Have an army stronger
Than yours, who will one day
Wipe you out
COMPLETELY
I truly believe you will be no more.
I'm releasing everything
And opening up to the
World to embrace

Love and to give love

Serenity POWER
Courage POWER
Wisdom POWER
I am now EMPOWERED
I am a HERO, helping HEROES.

H.E.R.O.E.S.—
Helping to **H**eal
Women and survivors
Educating and **E**mpowering
Women and survivors
As we walk hand in hand with
Women and survivors to
Regain self-**R**espect
Overcome **O**bstacles
While **E**ngaging and **E**xciting
Women and survivors with
The **S**trength to **S**urvive.

YES, WE ARE HEROES.
We are that army that
Will NEVER QUIT
We are that
Army that will endure
We are
That army that will be
EMPOWERED
We ARE
Faith Empowered Women.

Now as I continue on this
Journey called life, this
Journey to greatness, I will
Daily decree my freedom
And declare it to be
Not only for me, but for
Every other woman that
Has been touched by YOU, little c
We WIN in the end.

I Declare and Decree:

I am strong. I am vibrant. I am healthy. I am FREE. I am a victor. I am liberated. I am whole.
I am balanced. I am EMPOWERED. I am faithful. I am beautiful. I am stable. I am driven.
I am a FIGHTER. I am grounded. I am HEALED. I am smart. I am LOVE.
I am a S U R V I V O R. I am a giver. I am BELOVED. I am an encourager. I am positive.
I am active. I am covered. I am an OVERCOMER. I AM feminine. I am caring. I am capable.
I am secure. I am purposeful. I am nurtured. I AM sexy. I am living. I am open. I am wise.
I am peaceful. I AM a WOMAN. I am a HERO. I am POWERFUL. I AM courageous.
I AM a WINNER. I AM… ME.

Teal Drop

Teal Drop.
It's a rock-solid journey
The dropping of tears…
The heartbeat, the fears.

The Teal Drop
in confidence,
In dreams and everything you once
Thought life would bring.

The Teal Drop
Of family, sadness and heartbreak
The look in their eyes due to
Your possible demise
No one can help you,
Or come to your rescue
Only their prayers and
The grace from God.

New life—
New dreams—
New friends—
New names.

Teal Drop
Drip. Drip. It makes me sick
Drip. Drip. I think this HAS to be it
Drip. Drip. Find another way
Drip. Drip. Drop.

Teal Drop
It's time for the ring day

Ring the bell to begin my
New destiny
The hours, minutes and seconds
Of praying and recovering from
The feelings, thoughts and words—
The pain, the trauma—stormy weather
Working in my mind—working in my body.

It's all about the Teal Drop
Of faith—the size of a mustard seed
Drop of encouraging words that keep me going
Strong and high like an eagle I saw
Today, flying in the sky.
Dropping old ways and habits as I go up—
Up—up and away to my destiny
Operating in my Superpower with
Strength, belief and a strong tower
That can't be knocked down.

Teal Drop—
YEP
It's a rock-solid journey
Like that of diamonds
It starts off dark and not so appealing.
But, as it goes through the process,
The beauty begins to shine—shine—shine.

Facing Fear

“Fear is an excuse to remain the same... to be comfortable.” These are words you would find my coach, Shontaye Hawkins preaching as she stretches her clients. I can tell you, I have held myself back for years for this very reason—to remain comfortable. It was not something I realized to be true, but indeed, it was true.

My stomach usually balls up and my heart races whenever I face something that's frightening to me. Overcoming fear, anxiety and facing the experiences and challenges that I needed to face in order to go to the next level, was something I was hungry for.

My accountability partner, Ericka Rhodes and a close friend, Eric Coffie, have both exposed my comfort areas to the point of me dreading to be the same anymore. I wanted more. I wanted to change.

Fear has kept me from reaching major goals and I can honestly say, I have comfortably moved forward at times until I was shaken to my core. There have been many days and nights that I felt I needed a jolt to my spirit. That's when I called on my favorite home training through the Youtube platform. When I needed a mindset shift, I plugged into the greatest in the field of personal and professional development.

Some great names include Les Brown and Tony Robbins. I've been blessed to learn from Les Brown in person through my Traci Lynn business. He's motivational and has given me a lot to think about regarding my life and business. Tony Robbins is an immersion transformation specialist. He does more than motivate. He teaches that motion creates emotion. Because I know what it feels like not to want to do something, when I listen to Tony, regardless of how I feel at that moment, I am driven into action. It is when I connect with their teachings that I feel excited and self-motivated to soar after my dreams and goals.

In addition to these international greats, I listen to the teachings of Dr. Traci Lynn, Eric Thomas, Brian Tracy, Valerie Burton, Dr. Lawana Gladney, and Delatorro McNeal, II, to name a few. I have taken their classes, read their books and have even been coached directly by some of them. You want to see lasting change in your life, this is what you must do, use the strategies and skills that work for you.

Change is birthed from desire. This is something that I have found to be a thread within my life as I had to pull, scream and scrap my way through. I have kicked and screamed out of my comfort zone to a place that stretched me and ripped me apart so that I could then be put back together again. Even when I failed, I got back up because I refused to give in to failure.

There are various definitions of success. For some people, just finishing high school earning a diploma is a success. For others, obtaining several college degrees makes them a success. Still, for others, it means having a lot of money. For me, success is when all of the possibilities that God has placed in my mind are met and goals are achieved. This means I have health, wealth, physical strength and peace of mind.

It's not how others view what my life should be like, but it's what I see. It's my passions that have to be fulfilled. One thing is for certain, I will not and cannot give up until I see it all come to pass.

Facing Fear

Shallow breathing
Heart racing
Mind playing an old record that tells me to stop
Don't go. You know... the red light special

Paralysis in my mind and body
The 'what if' game goes on and on
Who am I playing with?
Because they seem to always win.

Action
Forward
Take action
Move forward
I tell myself these things, over and over again
The music without notes continues on
How is it that it plays only when I'm alone?
Trapped in my mind—trapped in my zone
Nowhere to go, but up
That's what Les says
I'm inspired and I move
I put on Tony and listen to him teach me
And I immerse myself in it when
My mind needs to reset and refocus.

PARB is what I call it
Knowing I have the
Potential,
I then take massive
Action
This brings about positive
Results

That increases my
Belief in myself,
Which, in turn, increases my
Potential.

The cycle that Tony has mastered
It coincides with his OPA
Knowing that I must know my
Outcome and
Purpose then
I'm ready to take massive
Action.
These are steps I take when
Overcoming fear. This is how I reprogram the
Broken record that plays in my head
Fear then turns into Faith
Excitement
Energy
Hope
Courage
I'm then pushing through the brick wall
That once felt too hard. It crumbles
And softens to a loosely made
Foam.

Like the voice of defeat I once knew.
Defeat that I once bathed in
Made love to day in and day out
Now, I am moving upward to my destiny
Fearless—
Fearless—
Fearlessly me.

It's Possible

The days pass
Time waiting for me is only a dream
I can't see the visions of tomorrow
Because of the pain and sorrow
Of procrastination.

Waiting to move forward
Because of the words I used to
Believe to be true
Words that paralyzed me
Daily—daily—daily
Fixed in my mind like a broken record
I can't seem to find a way out.

So, I sit there
I think to myself
How did I get here?
Again and again—
And again, I sit there

My heart races and mind paces
Muscles tighten. I tell it to relax
And then again
Like a stubborn little toddler
Who won't give in, it goes back
To a fierce war.

Blood flowing rampant into a panic attack
I just can't stand it
And then
Life happens
And as if given a wish by

The genie himself, my life shifts
God opens the heavens and
I get answers to the questions
That I've pondered while I sat there
Dreams and goals flowing from my mind to paper
The words flow like ocean waves to the shore
I combine my efforts with passion
That's what I've learned happens
When I finally realize
It's possible.

Take a Moment and Reflect

What has kept you from moving forward to your next level? What excuses have you used that hindered you from faith-walking to your destiny?

_____

_____

_____

_____

_____

Which faith steps can you take to make your life go into the next dimension?

_____

_____

_____

_____

_____

_____

_____

Your Turn

Share a time when your life took a sharp turn or halted because you took a leap of faith or because you refused to move forward due to fear or lack of understanding of what to expect?

_____

_____

_____

_____

_____

_____

_____

_____

_____

_____

_____

_____

_____

Radical Faith

Hebrews 11:1 states, "Now faith is the substance of things hoped for, the evidence of things not seen." This faith that we must have can sometimes feel scary. When thinking about life's situations that have not occurred, we must hope for the best outcome. This is how we exercise the "now faith."

When I was going through my cancer journey, I visualized my healing every day. That was faith. Then there's the time that I ran out of gas and my car stopped in the middle of the road. I prayed I would not get hit as I pondered how I was going to pay for gas because I didn't have enough money. A stranger came to my rescue and not only helped me move my car off the road, but also put a half tank of gas in my car. Then there were the times when my income was short of what I was paying out, and I didn't know how my daughter and I were going to eat, have lights nor water. With God, it all worked out for our good.

It is because of times like these I have built my faith muscle and developed radical faith. Radical faith to me is believing and hoping to the point that the world will think you are crazy. This faith is crazy, uncompromising, far-fetched and revolutionary. Then, when God steps in and shows up, the evidence of His grace, mercy and favor makes this radical faith all worth it.

I learned that my faith was not for me. Building my faith was for my testimony that is to be a blessing to others. It is through my faith that I not only please God, but I also show the hopeless how to be hopeful. It is through the display of my faith and obedience that I show those who have been impatient in life, that there is a gift that will be received on the other side of what they are going through. It is through my faith that others will be set free to be true to themselves and know that it is all for God's glory.

My radical faith has taken me places while I sought after a closer relationship with God. It's vitally important to connect with a spiritual mother and/or father. I have had many in my life and I still have great relationships with them to this day.

During this season of transformation, there were several pastors and spiritual leaders that participated in my growth after facing cancer. One person poured into me for countless hours sharing scriptures and stories with me, even theology and biblical language. My hunger increased. One person watered my growth with their teachings on life, family and wealth. Another person fostered an environment where I could worship and grow from a babe to a mature Christian.

Through my faults, drawbacks and sinful nature, I have had arms to run to, shoulders to cry on, words of hope to receive, empowerment and affirmation transforming my thinking and understanding about who I am and where I am headed. I have also had spiritual mothers that are too numerous to count.

These women fostered me through tough conversations, breaking me into my greatness with accountability and truth. At the point in my life where I was seeking a higher dimension, one of my spiritual mothers, Ms. Phyllis, introduced me to a new covering. This covering has been a teaching of raw unadulterated Kingdom Word delivered in a way that I have never heard it done before.

The love, support and encouragement to be who God created me to be was so refreshing. I learned to be obedient to the voice of God, regarding who I let get close to me and into my ear. Just in the natural, we walk in different levels of spiritual maturity. Therefore, once you grow to another level in the spirit, you will need guidance along the way to help you on that level. Other Christian believers, the Holy Spirit, constant prayer and my Pastors, John and Elaine Lofton, have been that guidance for me. Some people take for granted their spiritual relationships. They are critical for the growth of Christians. The Bible provides believers with scriptures on godly counsel. Here, I list a few, and as they are read, I pray that they will resonate within your mind, heart and soul: Proverbs 11:14; Proverbs 19:20; Psalms 1:1

Thank You, Pastors

Thank you, Pastors John and Elaine Lofton,
Because of you I feel free to be me
Now I feel better
To walk in my ministry.

Thanks for repeating to me
That it's what God wants for me
It now flows like never before,
I'm able to impact, encourage and mentor.

I love you and am grateful, you see
This is what I've been waiting for
That's why God sent me to C-3.

My Prayer - 2 Kings 4:34

There's a radical faith
Where I must detach from the world,
Centering in on God, in it all and through it all

Super strength and power
As I wait, renew my strength, help me fly high
With You, oh, Lord.
Soar high and mount up with wings
As the Holy Spirit moves me
I run and walk in Your way
And leave my way behind.

I surrender all
I surrender all
All to thee, my Blessed Savior
I surrender all.

Resuscitation is what I need
As I am powerless without you
Cover me, God
Shut the door on everything that
Hinders your spirit from filling me up
As I pray to You, Oh God,
My flesh perishes, but my spirit grows on.

As you lay upon me…mouth to mouth,
Eyes to eyes, hands to hands
I know by Your presence as
You're stretching out on me,
I shall grow warm in Your Spirit—life fills me up
Lord, as I walk to and fro, keep me
Stretch out upon me not once, but twice

As I need Thee.

Pour Your anointing out so I can give once…
Twice-three times-four-five-six-
Seven times over
So, I'm open to receive more from You.

Oh, God, my radical faith keeps me and saves me
Oh, my soul is set free and delivered
Now I can go on and do Your will
The works You have planned for me
As my faith grows and becomes new in You
The special kind of faith
The radical faith I can only get through You.

Take a Moment and Reflect

Do you have Radical Faith? How do you exhibit your belief in God, knowing there is a power greater than life, and that it might seem strange to others?

_____

_____

_____

_____

_____

_____

What can you do differently to surrender your life completely to God?

_____

_____

_____

_____

_____

_____

What areas in your life are you trying to control? What areas should you be letting go?

_____

_____

_____

_____

_____

_____

_____

_____

_____

_____

_____

_____

_____

_____

_____

_____

Your Turn

Write out scriptures that you can use to increase your faith, strengthen your mindset to help you believe in you and your possibilities?

○ _____   ○ _____

○ _____   ○ _____

○ _____   ○ _____

○ _____   ○ _____

○ _____   ○ _____

○ _____   ○ _____

○ _____   ○ _____

○ _____   ○ _____

○ _____   ○ _____

○ _____   ○ _____

○ _____   ○ _____

○ _____   ○ _____

○ _____   ○ _____

Take time out for you and God

Make a decision today to spend more time focusing first on God, and then your dreams and goals. Take time out for you today.

Time I will spend with God each day: _____

Time I will spend writing out my dreams and goals: _____

Time I will spend planning my action steps to fulfill my dreams and goals: _____

Time during the week I will take action on my dreams and goals: _____

PART III:

YOUR JOURNEY

RECORDED

Journal Pages

Record Your Story

"When you stand and share your story in an empowering way, your story will heal you and your story will heal somebody else."
– Iyanla Vanzant

$\mathcal{D}ate$_____

_____

_____

_____

_____

_____

_____

_____

_____

_____

_____

_____

_____

_____

_____

_____

_____

_____

$\mathcal{D}ate$_____

_____

_____

_____

_____

_____

_____

_____

_____

_____

_____

_____

_____

_____

_____

_____

_____

_____

_____

$\mathcal{D}ate$ _____

_____

_____

_____

_____

_____

_____

_____

_____

_____

_____

_____

_____

_____

_____

_____

_____

$\mathcal{D}$ate_____

_____

_____

_____

_____

_____

_____

_____

_____

_____

_____

_____

_____

_____

_____

_____

_____

_____

*D*ate_____

_____

_____

_____

_____

_____

_____

_____

_____

_____

_____

_____

_____

_____

_____

_____

_____

_____

_____

_____

$\mathcal{D}ate$ _____

_____

_____

_____

_____

_____

_____

_____

_____

_____

_____

_____

_____

_____

_____

_____

_____

Date_____

_____

_____

_____

_____

_____

_____

_____

_____

_____

_____

_____

_____

_____

_____

_____

_____

$\mathcal{D}$ate_____

_____

_____

_____

_____

_____

_____

_____

_____

_____

_____

_____

_____

_____

_____

_____

_____

_____

_____

_____

Date_____

_____

_____

_____

_____

_____

_____

_____

_____

_____

_____

_____

_____

_____

_____

_____

_____

_____

$\mathcal{D}ate$＿＿＿＿＿＿＿＿＿＿＿＿＿＿＿＿＿

＿＿＿＿＿＿＿＿＿＿＿＿＿＿＿＿＿＿＿

＿＿＿＿＿＿＿＿＿＿＿＿＿＿＿＿＿＿＿

＿＿＿＿＿＿＿＿＿＿＿＿＿＿＿＿＿＿＿

＿＿＿＿＿＿＿＿＿＿＿＿＿＿＿＿＿＿＿

＿＿＿＿＿＿＿＿＿＿＿＿＿＿＿＿＿＿＿

＿＿＿＿＿＿＿＿＿＿＿＿＿＿＿＿＿＿＿

＿＿＿＿＿＿＿＿＿＿＿＿＿＿＿＿＿＿＿

＿＿＿＿＿＿＿＿＿＿＿＿＿＿＿＿＿＿＿

＿＿＿＿＿＿＿＿＿＿＿＿＿＿＿＿＿＿＿

＿＿＿＿＿＿＿＿＿＿＿＿＿＿＿＿＿＿＿

＿＿＿＿＿＿＿＿＿＿＿＿＿＿＿＿＿＿＿

＿＿＿＿＿＿＿＿＿＿＿＿＿＿＿＿＿＿＿

＿＿＿＿＿＿＿＿＿＿＿＿＿＿＿＿＿＿＿

＿＿＿＿＿＿＿＿＿＿＿＿＿＿＿＿＿＿＿

＿＿＿＿＿＿＿＿＿＿＿＿＿＿＿＿＿＿＿

＿＿＿＿＿＿＿＿＿＿＿＿＿＿＿＿＿＿＿

Date_____

_____

_____

_____

_____

_____

_____

_____

_____

_____

_____

_____

_____

_____

_____

_____

_____

$\mathcal{D}ate$_____

_____

_____

_____

_____

_____

_____

_____

_____

_____

_____

_____

_____

_____

_____

_____

_____

_____

_____

$\mathcal{D}ate$_____

_____

_____

_____

_____

_____

_____

_____

_____

_____

_____

_____

_____

_____

_____

_____

_____

$\mathcal{D}ate$ _____

_____

_____

_____

_____

_____

_____

_____

_____

_____

_____

_____

_____

_____

_____

_____

_____

$\mathcal{D}ate$_____

_____

_____

_____

_____

_____

_____

_____

_____

_____

_____

_____

_____

_____

_____

_____

$\mathcal{D}ate$ _____

_____

_____

_____

_____

_____

_____

_____

_____

_____

_____

_____

_____

_____

_____

_____

_____

_____

$\mathcal{D}ate$_____

_____

_____

_____

_____

_____

_____

_____

_____

_____

_____

_____

_____

_____

_____

_____

_____

_____

$\mathcal{D}$ate_____

_____

_____

_____

_____

_____

_____

_____

_____

_____

_____

_____

_____

_____

_____

_____

_____

_____

$\mathcal{D}$ate_____

_____

_____

_____

_____

_____

_____

_____

_____

_____

_____

_____

_____

_____

_____

_____

_____

_____

_____

$\mathcal{D}ate$_____

_____

_____

_____

_____

_____

_____

_____

_____

_____

_____

_____

_____

_____

_____

_____

Cervical Cancer Facts Revealed

Did you know?

○ Cervical cancer happens to be the only gynecologic cancer that is prevented by having tests and screenings through the commonly known Pap test. This routinely and necessary test is the most reliable and effective way of diagnosing and preventing cervical cancer. When found early, this type of cancer is highly curable.

○ Cervical cancer begins in the cervix, which is the lower, narrow end of the womb (uterus). The upper part of the uterus and the birth canal (vagina) is joined together by the cervix.

○ According to the Center for Disease Control and Prevention, the human papillomavirus (HPV) causes more than 32,000 cases of cancer every year in the U. S, with 80% of people coming in contact with the HPV infection in their lifetime. Children ages 11-12, can protect themselves from certain cancers later on in life, by taking the HPV vaccine.

Risk Factors

o One of the most common risk factors for cervical cancer is HPV that can lead to six types of cancer.

o Having sex before the age of 18, with multiple partners, or engaging in sex with someone who has had multiple partners.

o Smoking doubles the risk.

o Extended use of birth control pills.

o Having HIV or other immune diseases that prevents the body to fight off infections.

o Giving birth to three or more children.

o Exposure to Diethylstilbestrol (DES), a man-made form of estrogen prescribed between 1940 and 1971, to prevent miscarriages.

Early Detection

Cervical cancer can be detected early with vaccines and specific tests.

o   There are two HPV vaccines that protect girls and young women from the strands of HPV that cause most cervical, vaginal and vulvar cancers. These vaccines are recommended for girls and women 11-26 years old. The Pap test is still needed regularly for screening for cervical cancer. Boys and young men can also take the HPV vaccine.

o   The HPV test is a screening that women ages 30 and above can receive to look for HPV changes on the cervix. Often used with the Pap test, it provides additional information when Pap test results are not clear.

Prevention

When looking at preventative measures against cervical cancer, there are several things you can do.

o Protect yourself from contracting HPV by getting the vaccine, using condoms while engaging in sex, and have minimal sexual partners.

o Regularly go to the doctor to receive a Pap smear that will detect cervical pre-cancers and cancer.

o If you receive abnormal results, make sure to follow up with your doctor.

o Refuse to smoke. Smoking impacts your body's cells, therefore, it's harmful to your cervical cells. If you happen to get HPV, smoking increases your chances of getting cervical cancer.

The facts contained in this text can be found at www.cdc.gov/cancer/cervical. For additional information on cervical cancer or other gynecologic cancers, contact a medical professional. For resources and/or support, reach out to one of the organizations listed on the following pages.

GYN and other Cancer Support Organizations in Charlotte, NC

Buddy Kemp Cancer Support Center
242 S. Colonial Ave.
Charlotte, NC 28207
704.384.5223
www.facebook.com/pages/Buddy-Kemp-Caring-House/125378460877327

Fighting Cancer, Inc.
www.fightingcancerinc.org
443.867.2253
fightingcancerinc@yahoo.com
www.facebook.com/groups/121737722468

Lydia's Legacy
www.lydiaslegacy.com
info@lydiaslegacy.com
www.facebook.com/Lydiaslegacy1

Serenity, Courage & Wisdom, Inc.
www.scawinc.org
234.57.LALUZ (52589)
scawinc@gmail.com
https://www.facebook.com/scawinc

Teal Diva
www.tealdivanc.org
shannon@tealdiva.org
https://www.facebook.com/tealdiva

Other National Organizations

American Cancer Society
www.cancer.org
Cancer Helpline: 1.800.227.2345
www.facebook.com/AmericanCancerSociety

Centers for Disease Control and Prevention
www.cdc.gov
1.800.CDC.INFO (800.232.4636)
www.facebook.com/CDC

Cervivor
www.cervivor.org
info@cervivor.org
www.facebook.com/cervivor

National Cervical Cancer Coalition
www.nccc-online.org/
nccc@ashasexualhealth.org
1.800.685.5531
www.facebook.com/StopCervicalCancer

BIO

KEESHA "La Luz" CARTER works with women who are fighters and survivors on their cancer journey.  As the founder of Serenity, Courage & Wisdom, Inc., she has helped dozens of women to use the Creative Arts as an outlet on their cancer journey. She survived stage III cervical cancer in 2009, which was an experience that showed her that cancer, was far more than a personal journey; it was to be used to bless others. She realized her purpose and mission was to empower women to be transformed to the best versions of themselves. As an entrepreneur, speaker, coach and author, she strives to not only motivate, but to be a transformation specialist who impacts the lives of countless women across the globe.

Visit La Luz at www.laluzspeaks.com
Follow La Luz at
www.twitter.com/laluzspeaks
www.instagram.com/laluzspeaks
www.facebook.com/laluzspeaks

For serious booking inquiries, email La Luz at
booklaluzspeaks@gmail.com.